UGLY DUCKLING PRESSE :: DOSSIER

M / W
Copyright © Matt Longabucco, 2021

ISBN 978-1-946433-82-4
First Edition, First Printing, 2021

Dossier Series

Ugly Duckling Presse
232 Third Street #E303
Brooklyn, NY 11215
www.uglyducklingpresse.org

Distributed in the USA by Small Press Distribution
Distributed in the UK by Inpress Books

Designed and composed by goodutopian
Printed and bound in the USA by McNaughton & Gunn
Cover and interior images: *La maman et la putain* (1973),
used with permission from Boris Eustache

This book was made possible, in part, by public funds from the New
York City Department of Cultural Affairs in partnership with the
City Council. This project is supported in part by an award from the
National Endowment for the Arts.

MATT LONGABUCCO

M / W

AN ESSAY

on Jean Eustache's
LA MAMAN ET LA PUTAIN

M / W

A MAN WAKES WITH a start. Grabs his watch. It's easily in reach — his bed is a mattress on the floor. Beside him, a woman sleeps facedown, under thick bedclothes, arms akimbo, her features not visible. The man rises, sprays something over his face from an aerosol can (a French thing?), then finishes dressing in two (!) silk scarves and a snug blazer. A last look at the sleeping woman and he's out the door. But he doesn't go far, yet — just down the stairs to the next landing, in fact, where a neighbor answers his knock. He asks if he can borrow her car and she promptly agrees, but reminds him the turn signal doesn't work. She offers her own solution: "I never turn left." How much accommodation to what's broken, we might quickly wonder, is too much? Cars are like us, abundant and complex, entirely of their age, often beautiful, evident in their diminishments, unmistakable in their ultimate breakdowns.

TURNS OUT IT'S ONE of those Peugeots about the size and patina of a stylish bike helmet. Having parked along a boulevard, the man appears to be on some kind of genteel stakeout. He sits in the driver's seat wearing sunglasses with oval lenses, scowling over *Le Monde*. When he leaps out it's to waylay a group of four students, three of whom walk on while he blocks the way of the fourth, a woman who seems irritated by his unexpected presence. "I wanted to tell you, 'I've come to get you,'" he announces, parrying her annoyance with his imagined version of how their meeting would unfold. (My school French a dim memory, I rely on the subtitles—one of translation's anonymous genres, and all the more difficult to trust.) It turns out they were lovers, now aren't. He urges her to consider all the precious time they've already lost. *Temps perdu*, he even says— we're having a Proustian encounter. After someone leaves you, after the tether of commitment snaps, there's nothing left but this abstract, bloodless talk, and yet there's a duty to say it all, like washing the plates after a bacchanal. "You should have said, 'I expected you,'" he instructs her, as their conversation shifts to a park bench before they carry on to a café (only after she agrees to pay). "You know," he tells her, "I feel you in me so deeply, so near—I can't believe you feel nothing." "What novel do you think you're in?" she asks. Funny, this familiar tactic, to accuse the lover of living in a book or a movie, as if those forms did not flower from the soil of feeling and experience. And isn't this a movie.

JEAN EUSTACHE'S *LA MAMAN et la putain (The Mother and the Whore)*, from 1973, is a bit hard to come by, as Eustache's family has thus far prevented the DVD or streaming release of this or any of his films. I hadn't seen it in years. My girlfriend Rachel went home to Paris for two months, and as a way to commune in her absence we'd gone back and forth suggesting movies to watch "together," hitting play simultaneously in our respective time zones. She'd heard Eustache's film mentioned before, and was curious to see it. I told her I'd like to watch it again, too — but how? It turned out she'd obtained a ripped .mp4 from an acquaintance with a trove of obscure films at his disposal. At some level she knows, or could guess, that this acquaintance had once been a rival of mine, in a bygone romantic entanglement, but probably didn't give a second thought to asking him. The severity of one's own drama drops off so precipitously in the estimation of others. It was all so long ago. And besides, she and I are far from love triangles these days, unless we count, as our third point, the almost singular figure the past becomes, or on the contrary some unknown person who might walk out of the future — a possibility this movie is about to insinuate — with a timing so arbitrary it's indistinguishable from grace.

WHY WON'T THE WOMAN return to the man? Might as well ask, why does she hear him out all afternoon, when she has, by her own admission, another lover waiting, and classes to attend. Desperate, perhaps wondering if she'll ever quite decisively cut the cord of his devotion, he tells her, "The day I stop suffering, when I work it out, as you say, I'll have become someone else, and I don't want that. That day, we'll have lost each other forever." The novel he thinks he's in is *À la recherche du temps perdu*. This woman even shares her name with Proust's narrator's first love: Gilberte.

THE MAN IS ALEXANDRE, played by Jean-Pierre Léaud, who was 29 years old in 1973. He had already played many roles, including the character of Antoine Doinel—the filmic alter ego of director François Truffaut—in four films by the time he made *The Mother and the Whore* with Eustache. Truffaut had cast him in 1959's *Les quatre cents coups (The 400 Blows)* based on a sense of affinity with his own troubled youth. "Jean-Pierre," said Truffaut of his star, "seeks to hurt, shock and wants it to be known...Why? Because he's unruly, while I was sly. Because his excitability requires that things happen to him, and when they don't occur quickly enough, he provokes them." The director of Léaud's school warned Truffaut that the boy was arrogant and defiant. Truffaut found him brilliant and kind. The relationship was more than that of director and actor; Léaud grew up a double. He revised, even as he played, over decades, a version of Truffaut's past self.

LÉAUD IS MESMERIZING TO watch, compact and energetic, a cockerel. His masculinity, like anyone's, is an interpretation, a variation on a theme. I wince at its shrillness. He never stifles his egoism, and seems to only flash his vulnerability in order to periodically release the tension his overbearingness creates around him. But by this same token, he seems manifestly a little boy, and the women around him tasked with letting him perpetually remain one.

ALEXANDRE TELLS GILBERTE HE'S ending their conversation. It has exhausted him. He even touches his temples, winces, and struts away—his bellbottoms toll. Emoting, imagining, and persuading are labor. Like directing a movie. Léaud played a director, this same year, in Bernardo Bertolucci's *Last Tango in Paris*. Truffaut-like, his hands raised in two L shapes to frame a prospective shot, he sets out to evoke on film the magical childhood of his lover, played by Maria Schneider. But we understand him to be pretentious, overly sensitive, cut off from the animal energy that animates Marlon Brando, to whom Schneider is erotically drawn—and whom she finally kills, for the hopelessly tangled, twofold reason of being appalled by his lower social class and frightened by his violence. Bertolucci's movie, along with Eustache's, marked a distinct aftershock of the New Wave of French cinema, its exuberance now curdled to disillusionment, its hoped-for new forms—social, aesthetic—collapsed into wreckage. The rot is not only described, it is enacted: to film *Tango*'s most notorious scene, in which Brando anally rapes Schneider, Bertolucci changed elements of the script—telling Brando to use butter as a lubricant—without warning Schneider, denying her right to know what the scene would demand and violating both her person and her image. Schneider attributed her later drug use, and attempted suicide, to the trauma of her experiences with the film. The destruction depicted in these famously lifelike movies went beyond them, into the lives they consumed.

ALEXANDRE AND A FRIEND sit side by side at the café Deux Magots, looking out onto the street. Alexandre always talks fast and sits up very straight. He tells his friend, "I read all afternoon. I plan to do it regularly, like a job." But a moment later he's rushing off, until caught in motion by the flagrant gaze of a woman at another table. He passes, turns back to catch her gaze again, she's gone. He wheels around and she's marching off down the sidewalk, the fringe of her long black shawl swaying with each step. He jogs after her, says something, the scene fades. Now Alexandre knocks on the door of the same friend he'd left earlier in the café. All this rushing around will be familiar to anyone who has experimented with indolence, which is like standing on a frying pan as it heats. And begs the question, is one's real wish to be forced to leap into the fire.

WORTH REMEMBERING: WE'VE ALL had a callow friend, but they've also had us. We could be watching a film by Éric Rohmer, whose *L'Amour l'après-midi (Love in the Afternoon)* had come out the year before, and whose *La Collectionneuse (The Collector)* features an early scene exactly like this one, right down to the friend showing the protagonist a sculpture he's made (in Rohmer's film, a paint can so spiky with attached razor blades that it can barely be handled). I remember the friend with whom I first watched Eustache's film (and Rohmer's, for that matter), at *fin de siècle* Film Forum, and how our wish to be bright and experienced in those days was like a botched translation, since we moved through the world cavalier and insolent instead. Watching now, I sometimes feel that former self inside me, the way a tree might chafe at some never-healed deformation of its inner rings. Other times, I know it would be as perverse to identify with that self as it would be for a creature to drag around the shed husk of its molted skin.

THE PAIR DISCUSS THEIR mutual appreciation for Jack Daniel's. (Lacan, who was analyzing patients in Paris in 1973, called it the best thing he'd found in America.) Alexandre reports that he picked up a girl and got her number. They try to figure out what she might do for a living, but give up since, according to his friend, the modern leveling of social classes means that "maids, working girls, and bourgeois women" are now indistinguishable by any outward signs. Alexandre anatomizes his conquest: blonde hair, blue eyes, possibly a "big ass." It's almost idiotic to have to say what I anyway only half-believe: every viewer watches a different movie. But this movie—long, cyclical, increasingly claustrophobic—emphasizes more than most this fact of each being thrown back on our own idiosyncratic daydream. It is more suggestive than narrative, and in its silences the viewer is haunted by conversations and glimpses, arguments and affairs whose tone or texture the voices and gestures on screen seem designed to beckon from memory. He stopped for the woman, he says, because she saw him first. "She looked at me insistently. That beautiful myopic stare."

Everything in Alexandre's apartment takes place on the bed. He puts his boots on it while he sits reading the paper. And it isn't his apartment — it belongs to Marie, the woman asleep in the first scene. When she comes home from her shop, he tells her about how strange it had been that morning to watch Parisians bustle around in a way that strikes him as false, since the frenetic activity of the morning disappears at night. The life he surprised at dawn was too bound to the clock and the workday, he complains, not woven organically into the texture of the streets. He extols the honest sadness of Parisians. And tells Marie he picked up a girl. She doesn't react, or tries not to. After they eat, while she does the dishes, he tells her why he only ever washed them once: he decided afterwards that the useful feeling the task produced in him was "obscene." "You asshole, you know I love you," she replies indulgently. She has also indulged, it appears, whatever idea about relationships would not only lead him to pick up a girl but brag to her about it as if expecting a proud pat on the head.

HE'S FULL OF IDEAS. He asks her if she wants to go to the movies, only to subject her to a forcefully sarcastic reading, from the paper he's been carrying all day, of a synopsis of *La classe operaia va in paradiso (The Working Class Goes to Heaven)*, an Italian leftist film that offends him in its dishonesty. A movie whose synopsis seems like an uncanny counterpart to the one we are currently watching. Is this movie going to be honest? How will we know if it is or isn't? This continual movement between movies or novels and *life*—as a thing that supposedly can't be gleaned, without interference, from novels and movies. As Gilles Deleuze wrote of Proust, "It is only on the level of art that essences are revealed. But *once* they are manifested in the work of art, they react upon all the other realms; we learn that they *already* incarnated, that they were already there in all these kinds of signs, in all the types of apprenticeship." And André Bazin, father-figure of the New Wave, wrote that the photograph "allows us to admire in the reproduction the original that our eyes would not have known how to love." Novels and movies tell us everything about life, only we forget to remember that about them, and look toward life at precisely the moment we should be shaking a novel emphatically in the air, or ceasing all conversation to contemplate a movie in the dark.

IT'S EASY TO DISLIKE Alexandre in this scene. This movie was released the year before I was born. I could use it to chart a social construction of heteronormative romantic love from then to now: so much inherited, so much buried, so much mutated in the reproduction of images and words. The characters seem to treat it as an endless and exhausted battle all are obliged to fight, in the name of a once-glimpsed ideal to which each combatant adheres only in their individual, unspoken ways. And now? Between the genders lies a no man's land of distrust, irradiated and made impassable by the damage done—and disavowed—by the masculine. And yet, on either side, one sometimes hallucinates pockets of perhaps unprecedented tenderness, rare, queer, and in spite of everything.

"THE COMMENTARY ON A single text is not a contingent activity, assigned the reassuring alibi of the 'concrete': the single text is valid for all the texts of literature, not in that it represents them (abstracts and equalizes them), but in that literature itself is never anything but a single text: the one text is not an (inductive) access to a Model, but entrance into a network with a thousand entrances; to take this entrance is to aim, ultimately, not at a legal structure of norms and departures, a narrative or poetic Law, but at a perspective (of fragments, of voices from other texts, other codes), whose vanishing point is nonetheless ceaselessly pushed back, mysteriously opened: each (single) text is the very theory (and not the mere example) of this vanishing, of this difference which indefinitely returns, insubmissive"
— Roland Barthes in *S/Z*.

Typing out the passage, I feel his pleasure, the permission he gives himself, in extending this single sentence, a sentence that itself describes the vast, singular, interconnected text we find when we turn to literature and in which we confront everywhere the intractability of difference — simply, an angle of vision on the world that we ourselves can never take, since someone else already inhabits and asserts it — and which therefore occupies our fascination in its ceaseless roving and caprice.

EUSTACHE: "THE FILMS I made are as autobiographical as fiction can be." Like Truffaut, like Léaud, he was thought to have suffered an unhappy childhood. But that could mean so many things. The director was reticent about his youth. He was born in Pessac, in Gironde, France, to a working-class family. And was an autodidact, as we might guess Alexandre, so strange but strong in his opinions, also to be. Eustache made many kinds of films, including shorts and documentaries, sometimes revisiting the same material in different forms over and over again. His work habitually refused to honor any meaningful distinction between fiction and fact. He had two sons. He was in a car accident, and injured, and bedridden, and shot himself that same year, 1981. He was just shy of his forty-third birthday. As I write this paragraph, a few months from my own forty-third, I'm not in his situation, but I understand in a way I didn't—ten years ago, let alone twenty—how a childhood grows heavier in the heart, or how that revisited material starts to seem like it comprises the walls of a maze whose openings and escape routes have, without warning, been fused shut.

It's DREAMLIKE, THE PHONE — HEAVY black-plastic pod connected by a coiled cord to its bulky station. The stack of records: big square sleeves with luscious black disks inside. Two pendant bulbs of a lamp are breasts, or a pair of ripe fruits. The black-and-white of the film is inky, hair and eyes and leather boots are thickly dark, while the whites of walls and doors read as rich light grays turning murkier in the night scenes. Alexandre, adopting a combative expression, dials up Veronika, the woman from the café. Marie and Veronika — close, but not exactly an M and a W, mother and whore, those words we'll eventually have to reckon with. This first conversation is a classic dance: they're trying to make a date; each tries to signal that they both care about it and don't. They agree to meet Thursday at the Deux Magots. "Be there," she tells him. "I hate being stood up."

ALEXANDRE STOPS BY HIS friend's apartment, where a series of riddles are posed. First, the friend has stolen a wheelchair, "probably from some cripple," and sits in it while they talk. He plays a record by Zarah Leander, a singer whom "the Germans tried to promote after Marlene Dietrich left." The friend reflects that, "like all imitations, she's better than the original." Alexandre flips through a book about the Nazi SS and the pair snicker about the solemn captions he reads aloud from its pages. His friend instructs him to pick up a magazine in which an optical illusion is presented; Alexandre stares at a drawing of a frog, then stares at the ceiling and, to his delight, sees the afterimage of the frog there. It's all so childish. But the riddles remain. Why should a person steal a wheelchair, and fool around with what someone else needs? Why is the imitation singer better than the original? Why is a book about unspeakable horrors funny? How can an image be where it isn't? Alexandre tells his friend he's telephoned Veronika, who "pretended to be busy," and asks him to pretend to happen by the café at the time he's arranged for the date. The friend agrees, on the condition that there be no improvisation allowed. Alexandre must instruct him precisely on how to behave and what to say: he must direct.

Riddle: why write or read about a movie, rather than simply watch or re-watch it? Why talk about love when everything you say will be a lie or, at least, a coating or film that fails to adhere to the relation every time it plunges into the dark pool where it goes, of its own volition, to unpredictably evolve? Love, movies, and literature go on without us, beyond us, indestructible because continuous, reversible, interlinked at every point. Our opinions and tastes are petty resistances to such totalities. Zarah Leander "better" than Marlene Dietrich! Marlene Dietrich who played Lola Lola in *The Blue Angel,* who went to Hollywood and made a slew of classic films with Josef von Sternberg (and Fritz Lang, and Billy Wilder, and Orson Welles, etc), who spurned the Nazis when they tried to woo her back to Germany, who received the Medal of Freedom for her tireless work for the Allies, who bedded (among many others) Gary Cooper and Jimmy Stewart, John Wayne and Yul Brynner, not to mention, it's thought, Edith Piaf and even Dietrich's professional rival Greta Garbo. She said, "Most people who make movies are in real life a bitter disappointment. I, on the other hand, am so much better in real life."

WE'VE ALREADY MOVED ON to other films together, but I confess to Rachel that I've been re-watching this one. It's asking me something, or pulling me back. She's French. She was seeing the movie for the first time. She's a scholar of performance. Can she tell me what strikes her? She emails:

"On the 'new natural', that strange, relaxed modality of speech that you can't help but notice is the way characters in a Godard film, for instance, talk to each other: language which aims so purposefully at casualness and yet remains highly stylized with its often flat affect, always a little bit offset somehow from the situation. I was surprised to learn there was a term (of course) for this way of being/speaking that's all over those New Wave films. A critic writing for *Télérama* in 1974 came up with the phrase 'Nouveau Naturel' to describe the filmmakers, Eustache included, who espoused this tendency. It's connected to the mode of production, as well as to a kind of narrative realism. Marja Wareheime's book on Maurice Pialat (like Eustache, a new naturalist) describes 'new naturalism' as the 'cinema that adopted the programme of the Nouvelle Vague—small budgets, reduced film crews, location filming, personal stories rather than literary adaptations—but turned its back on Paris to focus on the lives and problems of ordinary people in the provinces.' Notably, she remarks, *Télérama* praised 'the apparent spontaneity and improvisational feel of these films as well as the fact that they open a window onto the lives of ordinary people and starred relatively new, young talents.' Of course, *The Mother and the Whore* doesn't take place in the provinces—far from it—and the actors are familiar to the point of overdetermination."

"IT'S CURIOUS," SHE CONTINUES,

"to observe this relay between the new natural's purported 'spontaneity and improvisational feel' and the way I experience it—slightly distanced, even denaturalized, because it is precisely a knowing performance for the camera. Strip the theatrical of its stage and artifice, but hold onto its mimetic affect, and you have something like the naturalism of Eustache. Liveness, pulled up to a looking glass, is deployed to appear in all its casualness, but the question of what is natural and how that is even made visible is always on the line. Improvisation is where the natural cleaves. For some characters, improvisation is inadmissible. (Alexandre's friend: 'I'll do whatever you want, but I need everything to be pre-arranged. I don't do things casually. So, you decide if I should sit, stand, speak, or be silent. Improvisation is out of the question. If you want me to speak, tell me what to say. I'll say whatever you want, whatever you need me to say. I will recite it. Don't expect anything else from me.') For others, it is precisely what constitutes the film as such. Improvisation stretches out the time of the film because speech—and the speaking subject—is materialized through the time film takes. In the new natural, real time and reel time collapse into each other, and any scene might threaten to play on indefinitely."

AT THE CAFÉ, IT'S not Veronika who shows up but Gilberte who walks by—by chance, she says, though Alexandre will later declare, like a mystic or a psychoanalyst, that there is no such thing. She accepts Alexandre's invitation to sit and, questioned by him, admits she's marrying in a month. He tells her he'll just have to wait until she's divorced in "five or seven" years' time. He regrets his "one mistake," as yet unspecified, then tells her she's playing a role, points out how convenient it is that she's found a future executive for a groom rather than "a Portuguese laborer, or an Algerian." He compares their own relationship to May '68 or the French Occupation, and her subsequent engagement to France's resignation, in the aftermath of those upheavals, to disappointed mediocrity. He reminds her of an article he wrote about Michel Fauqueux—a reference I don't recognize. He suggests, monstrously, that she ought to bear a daughter whom, eighteen years from now, he could love in her mother's stead. Through all this, Gilberte listens, hardly reacting, turning her face away the one time he tries to lean in and kiss her.

I LOOK UP MICHEL Fauqueux. In October 1969, he abducted 3-year-old Sophie Duguet and demanded a ransom. When it was paid, he released the child but was caught and imprisoned. Alexandre fantasizes, as he speaks to Gilberte, about the child Sophie growing up and discovering, inevitably, the facts of the case. "A girl grows up, and already a man's in prison for her." Wouldn't she be waiting for him, he speculates, outside the gates, the day he was released? This isn't the last time Alexandre's thought experiments will tend toward the grotesque. Movies play in his head, he stages dramas and rituals. He wants to see what a fateful gesture looks like. But because he's lived through May '68, he fears that gestures fizzle. The openings in life — a sudden softness, a dangerous exposure, an opportunity won by virtue of the exact weakness that seemed to block the way — are sudden and brief, unpredictable and impossible to coax or court. Around them stretch expanses of melancholy made unbearable by the memory of those heights.

LIKE THOSE MOMENTS OF galvanizing intensity, in the weeks or months or years when, somehow, a rare concatenation of people collectively open a portal to a density and luster of meaning invisible and unreachable in the period before or after. *Meaning* absolutely everywhere—like on a street in Paris or New York. Such moments are ephemeral, and knowing this, one felt compelled to tell one's comrades, what we're enjoying now can't last, and so we should say "yes" to everything while affirmation is still possible. They didn't listen. They kept deferring, hedging, subjectivizing. Drenched in meaning, they assumed they'd never dry, though the sun was rising, though one gestured towards its appearance over the horizon like some kind of raving drunk. How to convince them, since one was oneself, in fact, incredibly drunk?

TIME'S A CHARACTER IN this movie (in every movie). Alexandre tells his friend he'll come over later, then in the next scene, he's knocking on the door. He tells Marie they'll eat later; the next scene finds them eating on the bed. Veronika says, let's meet Thursday. "Thursday's a long way off!" Alexandre complains. But we've learned that it's only a cut away. *Temps perdu* drains through the cracks in montage. Description and fantasy wage their cunning rear-guard action, with only partial success, against inertia and entropy. Eustache: "When the camera's on, cinema is happening."

THE PHONE AGAIN—HE USES it like a teenager. Shirtless: small muscular shoulders, small dark nipples. He leaves a message for Veronika, then reaches over and plays a record, leans back against the wall with his volume of Proust. I press pause: the cover reads *À la recherche du temps perdu,* volume five: *La Prisonnière.* QuickTime wouldn't play the subtitles, so I'm watching and pausing using the VLC app I sometimes use to download pornography, the better to obsessively watch and re-watch a minute of real time in which pure accident—the action of fluids, the reactivity of skin—erupts and undoes a performance and the attendant political reality of its making. A reality—as I know, but so often refuse to fully ascertain—whose apparatus operates just outside the frame and whose implied presence ensures the results have at least as much in common with investigative photojournalism as with the erotic repertoire, all within a given instant made uncanny by the fact of its arbitrary isolation from the absolute ocean of images of which it is only the most infinitesimal part.

HE CAN'T READ; THE song distracts him. The singer is Damia, the stage name of Marie-Louise Damien, the "third greatest" of the chanteuses (Wikipedia asks for a source on this ontic claim) after Piaf and Barbara (Monique Andrée Serf). The song, "Un souvenir," is the familiar claptrap about memory and dream, a beautiful and intoxicating past that can't be recovered. Léaud wears the convincing expression of enraptured thought he perfected as Antoine Doinel. Veronika calls back, asks if he's mad she didn't show up, he says not at all, can they meet, she asks him when he's free. "I can do what I want," he replies: the kind of thing one should never say in this world of ironic reversals, unless one is looking to be enslaved.

NOTHING CAN HAPPEN WITHOUT a doubling, a foreshadowing, an echo. Waiting at the café, Alexandre notices the woman sitting next to him, who does look an awful lot like Françoise Lebrun, the actress who plays Veronika. "Are you the girl I'm meeting?" he asks her. She says no, abruptly gathers her things and leaves, and he runs out in pursuit, nearly following her as she crosses the same way we'd earlier seen Veronika go. But he stops, a strange look on his face. Can he, as he has boasted several times now, do whatever he wants? Or has he just confronted, briefly and inchoately, the terror of a life truly lived that way, an existence made random by impulse and therefore never deepened by connection or development? A limit, glimpsed: where freedom is total, significance disappears.

SLINKING BACK INSIDE, HE identifies the real Veronika from behind and joins her at her table. He starts by commenting on the difficulties of talk. Wondering aloud how strangers make conversation, he makes it. "By not coming yesterday, you gave me that to talk about today. You've created something between us." Relationships, like history or the cinema, can only unfold by unfolding. He asks if he's boring her — Eustache may be worried, or only pretending to worry, that he needs to entertain us if we're to watch this three-and-a-half-hour movie in which people hang out in cafés or sit listening to entire songs play on records. In an interview, Eustache explains that it is through duration, rather than identification, that we experience the reality of his characters. We know each, he seems to say, in time, and because of time. And what we come to know, when we know each other, may be something about time itself rather than anything we might recognize in those others who travel beside us, and inquire of us as we do of them what came before or after the changes that arrived inevitably, and were somehow also impossible to provoke or predict.

OR IS IT ONLY me who perceives duration as an apparent stillness containing, unseen, a ceaseless internal churning, as when a child, now grown, spends a long and seemingly placid afternoon amongst the family who once terrorized him, all the while silently undergoing a torture that calls on all the senses, introjecting physical discomfort that could never be scratched, scraped, or squirmed away even while projecting, on the screen of the mind, the loop of shame and humiliation whose legacy is alienation from time in its felt flow — give me anything, he thinks, but the present.

CHANTAL AKERMAN, WHO SURELY felt the present's rawness (and filmed a version of *La Prisonnière*), said in an interview, "The most important thing we have in life is time. And duration. When they say that time flies, or I did not notice time, I feel they have been robbed. When you listen to music, cinema...it's very important to feel duration. Duration is given to you, you feel like you are living."

No one could be mistaken for Veronika. Lebrun's sad eyes take in Alexandre without betraying her estimation of him until, miraculously, she smiles a delighted smile. She enjoys him. We realize: he's enjoyable. He offers to talk about something else: the weather, Women's Lib. "What's that?" she asks. He lights up, explains that it's a movement of women who don't want to serve men breakfast. She considers this for a moment. "I like bringing a man I love breakfast in bed." Eustache admitted he wanted to scandalize and provoke the self-satisfied leftists he saw everywhere (was it really him in the guise of that neighbor, loaning her car, who found it expedient to "never turn left"?). Veronika draws a self-portrait: despite her German last name (Osterwald), she's Polish; she's an anesthetist at Paris's Laennec Hospital (lately refurbished as the offices of Kering and Balenciaga) where she lives in a garret; she has little money but likes to go to nightclubs and dance with men. "I'm easy to pick up, as you know." They make a dinner date.

AT HOME, ALEXANDRE TAKES a call from a man named Phillipe, who's looking for Marie. In the next scene, he's in bed with Marie, the man calls again, she answers and talks to him while Alexandre lies listening with his back to her. Finally, a third scene, he's giving vent to his jealousy. Alexandre and Marie swig from a bottle of J&B. They're fellow travelers, as Léaud was with Bernadette Lafont, the actress playing Marie, who by this point had been in films by Truffaut, Claude Chabrol, Jacques Rivette, and Louis Malle. Alexandre's a hypocrite—as he interrogates Marie about Phillipe, she reminds him of the nights she sat waiting up while he went out with Gilberte, then asks how things are proceeding with "the nurse." Midway through the drama, they laugh and kiss passionately. Unclear, at this point, to us, possibly to them: are they locked in mutual persecution? Or open to a polyamory that actually excites and enlivens them? Alexandre leaves for his dinner with Veronika.

I READ ALL THE articles on Eustache I can find online and experience a familiar writerly panic attack: everything's already been said. Almost everyone calls *The Mother and the Whore* a masterpiece, the culmination of Eustache's concerns, and a bleak vision of the aftermath of '68. Claire Denis and Olivier Assayas cite him as an inspiration; Jim Jarmusch kept a framed photo, above his writing desk, of Eustache on the set of this "beautiful, complicated film" we're watching. I discover Pauline Kael's 1974 homage: "It took three months of editing to make this film seem unedited." A eulogy for Eustache tells the story of a retrospective of his work held in Morocco. The writer, Serge Daney, imagines the heavy film canisters—there would be many for this long movie—being painstakingly loaded and shipped to the event. Then Eustache, invited but not confirmed as a guest, surprises everyone by showing up, and spends two days looking at the body of work he'd soon seal with his suicide.

AND I DISCOVER I'VE missed by a year a retrospective at New York's Metrograph, where I might have seen *Le Cochon (The Pig)*, the short film in which Eustache and his co-director Jean-Michel Barjol record in documentary fashion the slaughter of a pig. Or 1974's *Mes petites amoureuses (My Little Loves)*, the follow-up to *The Mother and the Whore* and an impressionistic record of the director's youth. And I won't catch *Une sale histoire (A Dirty Story)*, a pair of shorts from 1977 in which the same tale — regarding the use of a peephole from a men's bathroom into a women's one — is told twice, once as a monologue and again as a fiction. I'm heartened to know that Eustache was interested in repetitions, that he might have welcomed a book in which his movie is re-presented, in which a voice both embalms and reanimates the object and investigates the process of translation between forms — as slippery as the communication between those obscure galaxies we refer to, for convenience's sake, if you'll forgive the Proustism, as other people.

MORE THAN A FEW of the critics who write about *The Mother and the Whore* struggle to reconcile the movie's power and allure with its seemingly reactionary politics and its bleak view of a world in which sexual liberation has led to emptiness rather than fulfillment, and political dreams have washed back ashore to decay in the shriveling glare of individual shortcomings and social deadlock. I am holding on, so far, to the twists and turns in the story of these people who are ambivalent about each other but also determined, as their maker claimed, to "try to destroy each other." I'm ambivalent about them, too. They can't figure out how to be together, and they fake or recall—but can't really find—any lightness. I like lightness, and worry it's more necessary than I sometimes think, but I can't often find it. Where does it disappear to? I'm aging, is that it? Or is everything about sex, the city, the future really so grim? I suspect I'll have to say, eventually, what a livable life might look like without this pretense to charm and romance French movies sold so well that it can be hard to imagine what our desire would look like stripped of their (chic, forever modern) garments. I'll move, like a movie, to the next scene.

IT'S AN EPIC DATE. They meet at Deux Magots. How free, each asks, is the other, really? Alexandre defers. Veronika says she's recently left someone. "I cheated on him. I'm very demanding. I always expect too much, and I'm always let down." Alexandre describes a previous relationship in which he lived entirely at night, "drinking, gambling, making love," and eventually lost track of the woman he was living with, who led her life in the daytime. Bored at the "chicken coop" of the café, they move on to a restaurant at the Gare du Nord, which Alexandre says he finds cheering because all the people around him are in transit. "Like an F.W. Murnau film. F.W. Murnau films are always about transition from city to country, day to night." He asks again if he's boring her. She asks if she looks bored. "No, but women are such liars." (Eve Sedgwick on Proust: "The narrator frequently describes his possession of Albertine as suffocatingly boring to him. And then there's the issue of *her* boredom: whether it's his fear, his delusional fantasy projection, or his well-founded intuition...") He pulls out and reads from a self-portrait (an example of Alexandre's ventriloquism — the lines are actually by the writer Jacques Rigaut). He tells Veronika about a Borges story in which a sect of heretics locates ecstasy in boredom, in "the void." He asks how her food is. "Eating cold things," he muses, "you taste the cold, not the flavor. When you eat hot things, you taste the heat, not the flavor. When it's something hard, it's the hardness. When it's liquid, you feel the liquidity. So, you have to eat lukewarm, soft things." She laughs her lovely laugh.

WHAT'S A NURSE'S LIFE like? Repetitive, she reports. Nights at home she watches TV and showers, down the hall, while the news is on. He's surprised she doesn't watch the news. "Things don't matter much to me," is her blunt explanation. When she goes out to a nightclub, she takes whoever approaches her. "I can fuck anyone." But it doesn't last long. "I turn a lot of people off." Alexandre considers this, and answers, wonderfully, "That's normal." "My neck and shoulders are soft," she says. "I have pretty breasts. And I don't like thin thighs on girls. Do you?" It's a detached appraisal, as if from without. She might as well be calling herself a lukewarm, soft thing.

THE FRENCH NOVELIST MARIE Darrieussecq writes of the painter Paula Modersohn-Becker:

"In Paula's work there are real women. I want to say women who are naked at long last: stripped of the masculine gaze. Women who are not posing in front of a man, who are not seen through the lens of men's desire, frustration, possessiveness, domination, aggravation. Women in the work of Modersohn-Becker's are neither coquettish (Gervex), nor exotic (Gauguin), nor provocative (Manet), nor victims (Degas), nor distraught (Toulouse-Lautrec), nor fat (Renoir), nor colossal (Picasso), nor sculptural (Puvis de Chavannes), nor ethereal (Carolus-Duran). Nor made of 'pink and white almond paste' (Cabanel, whom Zola made fun of). With Paula there is no getting even at all. No sign of rhetoric, or judgment. She shows what she sees."

A PAST LOVE ON Instagram. The romantic scenarios she concocts. Precisely how she changes with time. And then, every so often, an image that seems out of order: a flush of youth, or a trick of light. Her distinctive voice is absent, of course. I recall it now only in dreams, where her avatar remains convincing. And yet somehow the idea of her voice is there in the photos, in the smile or else the sternness behind her eyes. I'm afraid I once felt exactly like the villainous neighborhood mafioso Michele Solara, in Elena Ferrante's Neapolitan novels. Solara's wife speaks with chilling clarity of the love her husband harbored for the narrator's brilliant friend Lila: "He didn't want her in order to have sex with her and then forget her. He wanted the subtlety of her mind with all its ideas. He wanted her imagination. And he wanted her without ruining her, to make her last. He wanted her not to screw her—that word applied to Lila disturbed him. He wanted to kiss and caress her. He wanted to be caressed, helped, guided, commanded. He wanted to see how she changed with the passage of time, how she aged. He wanted to talk with her and be helped to talk. You understand?" He claims, above all, to have *"recognized her."* Ferrante describes perfectly an obsession that must repel her to the core. Her heroes Lila, Elena, and Nino are a kind of flipped-over Veronika, Marie, and Alexandre. They too find their politics offer little protection against passions, degradations, and the license—flagrant, devastating—assumed by men.

PEOPLE SIT IN CAFÉS in order to regard themselves as in a movie—hence, the mirrors. To see themselves as doomed, as in American noir, or to relish that doom, by way of the noir-relishing New Wave. Another café, they drink whiskey and smoke, my throat goes dry just watching. Veronika dilates on life at the hospital, where interns and doctors are always coming on to her. One tricked her to get her alone. "So I took out my Tampax, fucked him, and went back to work." Veronika nonchalantly defuses the tensions by which power operates. Fascinated, Alexandre tells her he's always found nurses to be without compassion. He likes this about them. He tells her excitedly about a friend's scheme to find a surgeon to amputate this friend's right hand and display it in a jar of formaldehyde with a plaque: "My Hand, 1940-1972." Joking or serious, they take themselves or others apart. When they get up to leave, the camera lingers long enough to watch the next patrons take their place. Everyone's interchangeable.

THEY WALK BY THE river, an inky backdrop with points of white light. When they're about to part, Alexandre tries to put some words about love in Veronika's mouth, but she doesn't quite comply. "I'm often in love," she tells him. "I get involved with people quickly, and forget quickly. People don't matter. I love someone a month, two, three months, and that's it. When it's good, it's good. Then it's over." He kisses her, she goes inside. A graffito on the wall behind them—I read it as militantly feminist—depicts, on the left, a female sign above which is written, "avant." On the right, under the word "après," the handle of the mirror has moved up into the circle: it's become a crosshairs.

PROUST'S NARRATOR MARCEL, LIKE Alexandre, is a dandy and a know-it-all, and no one could be more cold-blooded, hoping his grandmother won't get sick because if she does he'll miss seeing Gilberte in the park that day. He can't help idolizing old France, and he worships a past of aristocrats and their storied names, while the family maid is a source of comedy for her malapropisms and narrow judgments. But Marcel the flawed character is not the author of the novel, the one who sees those adventures and obsessions from a lofty height, its atmospheres parted to expose a seam and a path. "That lie" between our lover and ourselves, writes Proust in *La Prisonnière*, is "one of the few things in the world that can open windows for us on to what is new and unknown, that can awaken in us sleeping senses for the contemplation of universes that we should never have known." Distrust is a dynamo, throwing off furious psychic energy, opening obscure portals. Marie is waiting up for Alexandre. She stubs out her cigarette and rolls over in the bed when he comes in. Revolted, she says he smells of Veronika's perfume (its apt and priceless name: Bandit). She tells him she walked the streets looking for him. This time, she's the one imagining scenes. She pictured finding him and saying, "I love you, stop this game, you'll ruin us." These characters exhaust me, and in their thrall it seems that echoes of such scenes are all I can remember of my own life, of all the kind and thoughtful people I know who get restless or jealous, who wish they were more free or equal, who feel the irresistible gravity of a void beneath them, and to whom, at least on some days, though it would be even more taboo to say so now than it surely was in 1973, nothing and no one really matters.

IS IT A GAME? Talk of love's gambits and rituals recalls Barthes, whose *S/Z* beckons despite the near-impenetrability, to me, of its structuralist vocabulary, and the frustrating indulgence of its longueurs. In it, Barthes sets out to anatomize Balzac's "Sarrasine," from 1830. The story's narrator is at a ball, and the woman he's brought as a guest notices a mysterious old man who sometimes haunts the home of the wealthy de Lanty family. The narrator proceeds to tell the woman about this old man. The tale concerns a talented young sculptor named Sarrasine. Trained in Paris, Sarrasine travels to Italy, where he sees an opera starring the singer La Zambinella. Sarrasine falls in love with La Zambinella and begins frequenting her performances. She is his ideal, he sculpts her, and soon tries to seduce her at a party. La Zambinella resists, hinting at a dangerous secret. When Sarrasine encounters La Zambinella again, she is dressed as a man—and is, it turns out, a castrato. Sarrasine refuses to believe this, but soon abducts Zambinella and confirms it, then tries to kill him before the guards of Zambinella's patron rush in and kill Sarrasine instead. Zambinella, we finally understand, is the old man from the beginning of the story, and was once the model for the portrait of Adonis that hangs in the de Lanty's home.

BARTHES'S INTEREST IN THE story revolves around its coded structure, the fact that it pushes toward an enigma whose solution it defers until the end: the enigma of Zambinella's sex. Sarrasine is undone by it. He loves Zambinella. When Zambinella's sex is revealed, Sarrasine's understanding of the world—the world in which his desire operates— shatters. It intrigues Barthes that the key to the enigma is an absence: the site of castration. It's hard to know what to do with the centrality of castration in psychoanalytic thought. To find that theory compelling is to do a lot of backtracking from its masculinist hysterias. But, like Eustache perhaps, part of me understands that legacy of discomfort and fear, if only because I respond deeply to that narrative structure in which the very thing that one has supposedly outgrown or dismissed returns with a vengeance. If the picture of gender relations in *The Mother and the Whore* seems outmoded and retrograde, nevertheless it threatens to come crashing down, upon some fraught and agonized moment, like a ton of bricks.

IT'S DAYTIME. HE COMES in; Marie's sitting on the bed with her back to him. She informs him frostily that Veronika's been calling. Marie's wearing a black silk shirt and black pants, and it's hard to resist the thought that she's dressed herself to rival the phone. It rings, she answers, it's Veronika again, Marie hands the receiver to Alexandre but then uses a kind of extra earpiece attached to the telephone by a second cord—a French contraption of the era, perhaps. She eavesdrops as they make a date, then asks him why he wants to go. What should he do instead, he asks her, "Stay here, watch TV, listen to the radio, wait for a phone call?...I'm a poor, mediocre young man. A poor, mediocre girl wants to see me. I like that, and I won't give it up, no matter what happens."

I WONDER IF ALEXANDRE really thinks of himself as a poor, mediocre young man. Certainly, he doesn't. He isn't. But also, in strictly material terms, the very terms '68 might insist we acknowledge, he is. And yet he is privileged to think of himself, despite his demonstrable poverty and mediocrity—he lives off Marie and does nothing all day—as romantic in his suffering and his condition. He has, in other words, submitted completely to the allure of French New Wave cinema. Its sumptuousness supplies him a convenient arc, posture, and rationale. What would I and all those past friends and lovers be, in this miserably expensive and inhospitable city, if we weren't revolutionary poets, dressed in vintage black and gloriously unlucky in love? It feels like we are alert to capitalism's delusions in every way but this—and yet, is this romance we can't relinquish precisely the lynchpin of our abjection? What would we be without it? A 200-year-old question.

AT THE CAFÉ, ALEXANDRE runs into another friend (this friend, played by Eustache's friend Jean-Noël Picq, looks a lot like his other friend. Both look like Eustache). Like his other friend, this one rattles off a series of compact allegories. He is wearing ill-fitting clothes, he says, because a large, intimidating salesman made him submit to buying them, and now he will have to get skinnier if he wants to fit into one jacket and fatter to fill out another. He bought an album of Jacques Offenbach's opera *La Belle Hélène*, then ran into a curious woman he knows, but she failed to ask him what he was carrying, and when he asked if she'd like to know she said she didn't care, and when he told her and offered to play it for her, she said no, she "didn't give a shit." So he listened to it alone. He ran into their mutual friend Freak, who was wearing green shoes, shirt, pants, and hat, and "even smoking green Gauloises." When asked how he was doing, Freak replied that it was obvious: "I'm in green, and against everything!" (The joke relies on a French pun between *en vert*=in green and *envers*=against.) The friend admires this and realizes that, because he himself is dressed in black, a similar statement on his part wouldn't mean as much. Does Alexandre take in these lessons? It's easy, says the story of the jackets, to be bullied into one's decisions, but the conclusions to which they lead may turn out to be diametrically opposed. It can be impossible, says the story of the opera record, to convince others to play the role we believe defines them (the opera tells the story of Helen of Troy, who can barely breathe from all the fatedness moving through and around her). It's conspicuous and definitive, says the story of Freak, to rebel. It's worth doing right and in one's own, playful way.

ALEXANDRE ISN'T HAVING MUCH fun, he's wavering, he looks glum as he notices and joins Veronika, who asks him what's wrong. "If I bother you," she tells him, "tell me to take a walk—it won't be the first time." I once loved a person who said things just like this, who asked me, when I momentarily excused myself in a restaurant, if I was actually going to sneak out the back—"others have, you'd be surprised." I remember perfectly the silence that used to follow, in which I saw that I was being invited to declare my devotion even though I knew that such an overture would only heighten the anxiety she was already expressing, and imagined was scaring me off. And so there were no terms outside the sphere of this game in which my avowal could function, however ready I was to offer it. And worse: at some level, it was my game too.

VERONIKA DRINKS RICARD, ALEXANDRE orders J&B. He's too broke to take her anywhere, he says, but we quickly understand it's a ploy to shift the situation, since the solution he proposes is that she come up to Marie's apartment to eat and watch television. He tells her she can leave if she doesn't like it — a basic right, he proudly adds. She smiles at the idea, assents. She can hold a highball glass with her thumb and two smallest fingers while her index and middle finger clip tight a cigarette.

HE'S CALLED AHEAD, THEY go up, Marie wears a rictus of a smile during an impossibly awkward introduction, then goes to the kitchen while Veronika settles in on the mattress and pours Coke into her whiskey. Alexandre puts on Marlene Dietrich, who sings in English: "I often stop and wonder/Why I appeal to men/How many times I blunder/In love and out again/They offer me devotion/I like it, I confess/When I reflect emotion/There's no need to guess." The scene cuts before the chorus can start: "Falling in love again/Never wanted to/What am I to do/I can't help it." A partial list of artists who have recorded this song: Ruth Etting, Benny Goodman, Zarah Leander, Billie Holiday, Doris Day, Sammy Davis Jr., The Beatles, Nina Simone, Linda Ronstadt, Ute Lemper, Marianne Faithfull, Bryan Ferry, Christina Aguilera. I like covers, obviously. I'd been working on an original story but then realized there was a perfectly good one just waiting around, in this movie, to be performed anew.

RIGHT AWAY, THEY'RE IN the car, looking dour, trying to figure out what to do next. A lot of "Si vous voulez"—they don't say "tu." (I still try to keep my ear on the French. What are the subtitles content to gloss over, what don't they bother to include?) Rachel tells me there was a push to do away with such formalities after '68, especially in the schools. But did it sound odd to her, while we watched? Yes—strangely distant. A grasp at social cohesion. A piety, even if only about the solemn importance of cinema itself.

They return to the Seine, Veronika says she's furious, a moment later she kisses him and tells him she's been having erotic dreams about him. All her feelings are at the surface, now. Alexandre retreats, and sulks. When she offers to make love to him right there, he demurs: "We're being watched." She tells him she doesn't see anyone, and asks him who's watching. "Voyeurs, homosexuals, cops." All his bluster, and now he's paranoid, prudish; in the next scene he'll ask Marie about her "dyke friends." He's a rebel dressed in black, but ordinary and hemmed in by banal and repulsive prejudices.

MARIE'S WAITING UP. "I don't like her! I don't like her face, her voice, her skin, her fat ass, her way of saying 'Easy, friends!' Disgusting!" She concedes, when Alexandre asks, that Veronika's breasts are nice, her "one good feature." We see Marie's, large with large areolas. She tells Alexandre to go ahead and fuck Veronika while she's away in London. In reply, he asks her to buy him a flannel suit while she's there, out of her pocket. He'll pay her back when he has the money. "There's no secret to flannel, it's all in the price." Then, as if it has just occurred to him, though he has already explored every imaginable variation on this theme, he tells her he wants a suit that will make people think him elegant and explains of everyday people, with an incredulous laugh, "They ascribe the elegance of the suit to the person. It all gets confused."

I FIND MORE ONLINE articles about Eustache in English while I wait for the NYU library to retrieve, from their offsite location, a book on the director — though it's entirely in French, which I can't really read. (Look, if all the books have been moved to a warehouse upstate to make space for conference tables and snack bars, then that warehouse *is the library*.) I skim the articles through the interstices of my fingers held over my face. I want to know more, but I also want to let the movie and my response to it unfold on their own terms. I find out from Pedro Costa that it was *Les cahiers du cinéma*, for whom he'd often written, that first called Eustache reactionary. Costa calls Eustache a "non-conformist whose films followed their material right to where it led them, and never to where conventional guidelines were pointing them." Another critic, Nick Pinkerton, puts the director in a lineage interested in old France and a "sexual counter-revolutionary" program that passes from Céline through Houllebecq. Pinkerton calls Eustache "an artist of great cultivation and erudition whose method nevertheless retained his blue-collar origins," and who "climbed down into the guts of his preoccupations and wrangled with them..."

I'M MOST DRAWN TO the details of process and biography Pinkerton includes, though his piece contains no notes (said the pot to the kettle) and leaves me stuck with only phrases and flashes. That Marie's apartment was actually Eustache's apartment. That the dialogue in the movie comes from "surreptitiously tape-recorded conversation-performances"—but to what extent, exactly? That Eustache really did date a nurse, Marinka Matuszewski (who has a cameo as the woman that Alexandre mistook for Veronika at the café). That Lebrun—Veronika—was Eustache's girlfriend for ten years, and that Marie's prototype was named Catherine Garnier (to whom the movie is dedicated, and for whom the part was written, though she didn't play it). That Garnier took her own life soon after seeing a rough cut of this movie, and that Eustache himself was the one to find her body, and suffered a breakdown in the aftermath. Pinkerton's truncated telling seems to imply that Eustache's movie precipitated Garnier's suicide, but no further information substantiates this potentially horrifying claim. I think of Schneider, after *Tango*. But of course the cause of our trauma is invisible—after all, it's forty feet high, and plays three times a day in every theater in town.

THE PHONE RINGS. IT'S morning. Marie's gone. Veronika apologizes for all the "stupid things" she said the night before, but Alexandre, either too self-absorbed or else tolerant because of his complicity, says he doesn't remember. He's to meet her at a café. She tells him she may be sitting with a man, but not to panic, it won't be a long meeting. When he arrives, she is in fact sitting with someone, but as Alexandre turns petulantly to go he sees a friend of his own and joins her instead. She's been away in New York, "an awful place" where, she tells Alexandre, "an amputee tried to pick me up. He wheeled after me, real fast, he looked mean, he said, 'Yeah, you won't go with me cause I'm an amputee.'" The characters' casual aggression toward the disabled, in this movie, barely conceals their terror of dependency, which is itself their fear of a future they don't do a thing to improve.

IT'S NOT ENTIRELY CALLOUS: the friend has a bandaged hand, and Alexandre—he often lapses into real tenderness—comments that it "makes a nice accessory." Wayne Koestenbaum, writing about Harpo Marx, admires Harpo's propensity for cutting everything in sight. "Scissoring, Harpo sweetens castration, makes it nonlethal, nontraumatic." Harpo "doesn't consider castration a problem," and neither does Koestenbaum, who likens his own interpretive zeal to a decorative snipping of the edges of things. Harpo is silent; Koestenbaum and Alexandre are verbose. Alexandre, unlike them, like Sarrasine, is dead serious. But Sarrasine is terrified by castration and Alexandre's saving grace—he needs one—is that he isn't. He's keen to be transformed, he just doesn't know how to effect the change. His one big idea is to switch places with someone, and he tells his friend about seeing a person they always called the "imitation Belmondo" (Léaud and Jean-Paul Belmondo are each a kind of double for the other) who perfected his imitation until "he was more real than the real one." My therapist's favorite trick, when I obsessed over someone, was to ask if I wanted to *be* that person. Sarrasine and Zambinella are doubles, too, says Barthes: hence *S/Z.* "If you really want to," Alexandre muses, "you can take someone's personality, you can steal his soul."

ALEXANDRE ASKS HIS FRIEND for news of their old crowd, who all abandoned him while he was sitting still, he says (tell me about it). One committed suicide, the woman tells him, then admits she botched her own attempt. A rival of Alexandre's died, which makes him happy. I love Alexandre's undisguised malice toward his rivals. He decides that everything in the world is against him. "There was the Cultural Revolution, May '68, the Rolling Stones, the Black Panthers, the Palestinians, the Underground, and for a few years, nothing." What a list, but what it means to Alexandre we can't quite say. Lost old friends had been the subject, but the moment they inhabited together must be what he misses, what died. His friend tells him that she's been thinking of cheating on her boyfriend. He tells her that if she decides to go through with it, she should call him up. Veronika comes over. He tells her Marie's gone to London. Would she like to come over? "Let's go. I want to hear that Marlene Dietrich record."

THE LIBRARY ALERTS ME that the book by Alain Phillipon has arrived. Rachel tells me I'd better learn French; it's a running line between us, but it makes me nervous, too—what if I'm too set in my limitations. I scan and send her some pages, and she translates a quote for me, or rather, one quote nested in another:

"Jean-Pierre Léaud often wears black sunglasses in the film which look very much like those Jean Eustache wore at the time. Shutters, a 'mask upon my passion' as Roland Barthes, wrote, a few years later (in 1977), in *A Lover's Discourse*: 'To hide a passion totally (or even to hide, more simply, its excess) is inconceivable: not because the human subject is too weak, but because passion is in essence made to be seen: the hiding must be seen: I want you to know that I am hiding something from you, that is the active paradox I must resolve: at one and the same time it must be known and not known: I want you to know that I don't want to show my feelings: that is the message I address to the other. Larvatus prodeo: I advance pointing to my mask: I set a mask upon my passion, but with a discreet (and wily) finger I designate this mask.'"

She adds:

"I look a little further along in Barthes' fragment, and find his description of the contradictory posture of the lover who, having cried, puts his sunglasses on to conceal his swollen eyes. Barthes writes: 'I want to be both pathetic and admirable, I want to be at the same time a child and an adult. Thereby I gamble, I take a risk: for it is always possible that the other will simply ask no question whatever about the unaccustomed glasses; that the other will see, in the fact, no sign.' Alexandre never wears his sunglasses inside, but it's inside that he most closely toes the line between child and adult, asking to be fed, housed, and clothed by Marie, and loved there unconditionally by her, while also asking to be loved, impossibly, by Veronika, the lover who gives him reason to posture, to self-affirm, to lie, even, so as to impress."

"I'M STRUCK," RACHEL WRITES,

"by how Alexandre's heroic pose (the monologues, the acting—what Veronika calls 'un maximum de cinéma'), throws us back onto a fundamental ambivalence—his subjectivity is as postured and performed as it is underwritten by an intractable dependency on these women. His 'mask,' his sunglasses, his acting, may conceal his suffering, but only to better draw attention to it. It's an endless relay; Philippon argues that the mask may be 'one possible metonym for the film, which functions according to a principle of oscillation and double-crossing.' It signals Alexandre's own paradoxical contingency of which we are reminded through these signs to which the film points: Alexandre hides, but vies for visibility; he isn't if not for the camera, if not for the audience Eustache has given him and his theatrics within the film itself."

A CONFESSION—I'M INTERPRETING THIS movie as a suicide note. If that's insupportable, I get it, I release you, you may stop, as many times while watching this movie one wishes to stop before enduring a minute more. A salient feature of the movies, almost too obvious to be named, but all the more powerful for that: they play until they finish. Of course, one can leave, or press stop, but otherwise they continue and end in their own time (unlike books, but very much like life). Truffaut called Léaud a provocateur, but Eustache's friend Jean-Jacques Schuhl found Eustache himself the opposite: passive, in love with nothingness, a director who said, "Things are there. Why manipulate them?" And yet, he took an action, even the action *par excellence,* when he stopped his life.

FINALLY: THEY'VE FUCKED. NAKED, in the bed, in the darkness, after. Rachel and I make fun of the way they kiss, a particularly uncomfortable- and false-looking face-mashing that stands in contrast to their otherwise naturalistic behavior. We take it to say, for the millionth time: there's nothing natural about talk, time, or sex. They start up again, hasty Alexandre accidentally pushes her tampon in, annoyed Veronika tells him he must reach in and take it out. He says he's afraid to hurt her, then fumbles, laughs like a schoolboy, and finally retrieves it. When she goes to the toilet, he tries to call his friend to tell him about the funny incident that's just occurred. Luckily, the friend doesn't answer the phone. Why so uncomfortable, Alexandre, you fucking twat? Castration looms, perhaps—a little thing disappearing. "You have beautiful veins," Veronika tells him, in nurse- or vampire-mode. "I'd like to give you shots." If only he'd let himself be the one to get fucked. Sometimes he seems so close to stepping outside the narrow masculinity he inhabits, but he never does, he's trapped by it, always tumbles back into one of those binaries that lead nowhere. He climbs on top of her: "How do you want it, tender or violent?" Another heresy against the cherished spontaneity of this act (not to mention the ostensibly inevitable unfolding of events we call a movie). She likes both, she says. In the morning she's gone, then she telephones, they make another date.

RIGHT AWAY THEY'RE IN bed again. Veronika, who's spent two nights at Alexandre's (Marie's!), recalls the last time she lived with someone. The man liked yogurt, so in a loving gesture she filled the fridge with 30 yogurts, which he found "a bit weird." "He loved yogurt, and wanted me to say 'I love you.'" Well, he's ancient history. They listen not to Dietrich but to Fréhel, whose life is a contender for the saddest among the French chanteuses, which is really saying something. She grew up on the streets of Paris, became an alcoholic at a young age, and attempted suicide at nineteen. Her career crested and ebbed in relation to her addictions and her heartbreaks. Alexandre and Veronika listen to "La chanson de fortifs," a deeply nostalgic song about a lost Paris. Veronika follows by singing a sad tune about a plucked rose. When she's done, Alexandre comes out of the trance she's created and remembers to turn on the radio to catch a bit of the Sunrise Preacher. He says he always listens to this never-varying program in which a preacher laments the lazy century and its degraded people ceding their bodies to sloth and their labor to machines. Alexandre compares this disembodied voice to "the man of June 18th," a reference, as far as I can tell, to Charles de Gaulle's speech, in 1940, to the people of occupied France, a gesture widely credited as the beginning of the Resistance. But wasn't de Gaulle himself the enemy, in '68?

IN HER BOOK *MAY '68 and Its Afterlives*, Kristin Ross quotes the militant leftist Pierre Goldman on a statement de Gaulle made during the demonstrations: "What he said was simple. In his pitiless discourse he recalled that the forces he represented, force itself, was capable of wars and history. He sentenced his adversaries to impotence and dream. To castration. It was a challenge and no one took him up on it. Power chased away imagination. The festival was over."

ALEXANDRE SUGGESTS BREAKFAST AT a restaurant where, he says, incredible people weigh their every word and speak like books. As evidence, he recalls overhearing someone else citing the comments of a colonial administrator on the sexual pleasure to be found among the local population. It's the fact that this was reported that seems to strike Alexandre: "To speak with the words of others...that's what I'd like. That's what freedom must be." And yet to weigh one's words, here, to speak like a book, and to find freedom in citation, is to ventriloquize the racist mentality of the colonizer. What kind of freedom is that? The freedom to stop caring about the humanity of other people. Alexandre plumbs the nadir of his cynicism and self-pity. Having once been among those who tried their best to dislodge the structures and histories that bind, he sometimes seems ready to throw in with all those who are shackled by them, or worse, prop them up. Algeria, along with collaborationist France, haunts this movie; racism and the complicities of the nation linger in its bones. The characters could never lay these phantoms to rest. They simply haven't the tools; there is nothing we've seen, in this landscape of drinks and cigarettes, blazers and dresses, beds and cafés, that might alter reality rather than simply rearranging it to a fleetingly enchanting effect. There is no other world to imitate. Any new reality would have to be generated from attending in some more precise way to this (miserable) one. Eustache: "What I said was it is necessary to render one's personality akin to a mirror in such a way that reality reflects itself in it."

BUT THE BIG FINISH is still to come: "One day in May '68...the café was crowded, and everyone was crying. A whole café, crying. It was beautiful. A tear-gas bomb had exploded. If I hadn't been going there every morning, I'd have seen none of that. But there, before my very eyes, a crack in reality opened up..." Alexandre is in tears, telling her this — tears, even from tear gas, are still tears. A believer, after all.

WHAT'S THAT "CRACK IN reality"? Alexandre antic-
ipates Deleuze and Guattari, whose essay "May
'68 Did Not Take Place" begins, like several of
Alexandre's monologues, with a list of historical
upheavals before addressing the titular crisis:

"The historical phenomena we are invoking were
indeed accompanied by determinisms or causalities, but these were of a peculiar nature. May '68
is of the order of pure event, free from all normal,
or normative causalities. Its history is a 'series of
amplified instabilities and fluctuations.' There were
many agitations, gesticulations, slogans, idiocies,
illusions in '68, but this is not what counts. What
counts amounted to a visionary phenomenon, as if
a society suddenly perceived what was intolerable
in itself and also saw the possibility of change. It
is a collective phenomenon in the form of: 'Give
me the possible, or else I'll suffocate.' The possible
does not pre-exist, it is created by the event. It is a
matter of life. The event creates a new existence,
it produces a new subjectivity (new relations with
the body, with time, sexuality, the immediate sur-
roundings, with culture, work). [But…] each time
it appeared, the possible was closed off."

"OR ELSE I'LL SUFFOCATE"—THE cry of the seeker after the possible. Eustache thinks often in terms of suffocation (as, of course, did asthmatic Proust). In a 1971 interview—before *The Mother and the Whore*—he describes a desire to break with the films he's made to that point "because they were suffocating me." His characters inhabit small, shabby spaces and chafe against the constraints of monogamy and work. Alexandre hangs out in cafés, picks up women, talks to them. Like him, to feel him, I summarize and digress, summarize and digress. I can't tell if I hope to stumble on an epiphanic kernel, somewhere, or if I'm only marking time—the time between events. Events for Eustache: childhood, '68, suicide. Moments where the self meets the void, where chance recedes but determination is likewise disabled. In the time between when I first watched this movie and when I watched it with Rachel, I married, had a child, got painfully divorced, died for love, revived for it, filled pages with poems and essays, stood at Ground Zero and Occupy. And when a would-be autocrat came to power, the Resistance mobilized, though a persistent and difficult-to-silence part of myself kept whispering, like Ken Kesey at the Berkeley march against Vietnam, not in the '70s but in the still-surging mid-'60s: don't fight the way they do, turn your back, just say fuck it, embrace existence as a nothing. Meanwhile, in the past few years, I've become attuned to suffocation, literally—I've had claustrophobic episodes, frantic panic attacks, breathless dreams so vivid that now I can call up the feeling they produce anytime, like calling a friend on the phone.

EUSTACHE, IN THAT INTERVIEW, seems restless and pained. He refuses to separate art and life, or leave them in their proper places. Of those previous films he complains, "I felt like I was always doing the same thing but, above all, it's less in relation to the cinema than in relation to myself that the problems were presenting themselves. Each film was making life more difficult. When I'd finished one, I was always thinking I was going to be able to see things differently, to live a little better, and it was the opposite that was happening, I was living worse and worse." Does he mean financially, asks the interviewer, Phillipe Haudiquet. Yes, that too. An insubordinate New Wave scion, Eustache keeps saying he wants to return to the static framing of the Lumières. He keeps camera movement to a minimum. He says, "if you shoot, you don't need to make a movie, it makes itself." He believes in expression by way of the mirror. Later: "It's always the films you do for personal reasons that innovate, and not the ones you do for technical or artistic reasons." For this sentiment alone, I love him.

AND WHAT AM I, and what can one be, an uptight rhetorician, a person who cares—near or far, focused or diffuse?—or a freedom-seeker, but then who does the dishes? *Ne travaillez jamais*, but who pays the rent? A somewhat resentful freedom-deferrer, then? An occasional sharer? A voice for radical compassion? But when desire hits? What novel do you think you're in. What film. Personal reasons. Sometimes I just want to fuck and feel alive, and sometimes I remember how that seemingly simple desire has led more than once to confusion, humiliation, and heartbreak. I wonder who I exhaust or overwhelm with what Rachel called, referring to Alexandre, my intractable dependency. Or is that the "boring and cruel" superego talking, what Adam Phillips calls the fixedly "accusatory character" who we would quickly walk away from, if we met him at a party? "We might think that something terrible had happened to him," writes Phillips of this imagined meeting. "That he was living in the aftermath, in the fallout of some catastrophe. And we would be right."

THE REVOLUTION WE'RE TRYING to live is haunted by the old ones, their blind spots, their cruelties, their romance. But scholar Wendy Brown, in her "Resisting Left Melancholia," laments a Left "that is most at home dwelling not in hopefulness but in its own marginality and failure, a Left that is thus caught in a structure of melancholic attachment to a certain strain of its dead past, whose spirit is ghostly, whose structure of desire is backward and punishing." This is the melancholia Freud described, in which a subject, denied its beloved object, preserves at least the ideal the object represented by reproaching, not the object, but himself. Walter Benjamin adopted this formulation to point out the fetishization, among leftists, of their own dashed passions. Brown says it is precisely this leftist, gazing backward, who becomes the most conservative, who can't understand that the political organization of the past cannot speak to a changed present that has been ceded to the opportunists who at least recognize the situation for what it is. The result: a Left "that has become more attached to its impossibility than to its potential fruitfulness…"

BROWN IS QUOTED BY Mark Fisher in *Ghosts of My Life*, a book whose publication preceded its author's suicide by just a few years, and which seeks to explore the "hauntology" of a time that cannot move forward from all its unfinished and unresolved business. May '68 was fifty years ago; I watch like it was yesterday, or tomorrow. Amazing that Eustache was able to see so clearly the melancholy that Brown describes, into whose deadlock he had arrived—not decades but just a few short years after that indelible heyday and touchstone of leftist action.

JEANNE MOREAU DIED TODAY, July 31st. She was 89 years old and, among her many roles, played Léaud's mother in *The 400 Blows*. Alexandre makes the bed by climbing around on top of it, pulling the sheets toward the corners. When Veronika asks about this method, he informs her that he saw it in a film: "Films teach you how to live, how to make a bed." He hasn't even changed the sheets. When Marie comes back, she's disgusted by the remnants of the love nest, and announces she's going to sleep in the other room.

THROUGH SMALL APARTMENTS, IN New York, in Paris, we maneuver the large spaces we carry within us. We can only report on our sojourns to these interiors, or fail to, when from a distracted moment our lover interpellates us with that habitual question, "What are you thinking?"

Rachel is amazed that Marie's tiny apartment suddenly expands, in this scene—and that this is the first we've heard of it:

"On page 111 [of Phillipon], there is a production photograph of Eustache, crouched on the floor and gesturing, mid-sentence, a cigarette in hand. He wears round, dark sunglasses. I recognize the room from the bottle of Coke, the glass of wine, the record player. It's a photo taken on the shoot of *La Maman et la putain*, in the room where most of the film was shot. The film took about four and a half weeks to shoot (so short a time for so long a film) and I can't help but imagine most of that time was spent here—in this room which, up until the scene in which a bedroom is revealed, seems to contain everything, serve all functions: bedroom, living room, dining room, study. Eustache was clear: 'Whenever something happens elsewhere, the scene ends and an ellipsis needs to be added in. In the next scene, the character recounts what we did not see. They tell the story. This is the film's preference: that everything should be told and nothing should be seen.' So we're always here, in this room. He shot with the camera down low to fit the seated or recumbent actors in the frame. It becomes hard, in this film, to imagine anything outside of this frame, these actors, the few locations we're brought to. This is why to see this photo of Eustache in the room is almost incongruous, at the same time as every scene shot in this room could not be imaginable were it not for his being there."

ALEXANDRE CRAWLS IN BED with Marie. She always forgives him, though she tells him she's wise to his "charming little boy" routine. Dark thought: this couple, like many, loves their argument most of all. Their mutual alienation is a dare. From the unstable world of their room, as Rachel suggests, everything is condemned to originate.

AND NOW ALEXANDRE MUST win back Veronika. Marie's return has made the division the lovers once took for granted into something more like a split. She waits for him, without waiting for him, at a table inside the café. Full of pride, he approaches first with his friend. The two men snicker about Sartre, whom they point out on the far side of the café and deem a drunk. Veronika's amused. They talk about women they've known who killed men (the friend we met, with the bandaged hand, is now wanted for murder, says the day's paper). Women who killed themselves. Or—to Alexandre, the same thing—women who have had abortions. He's speaking from grief, we'll soon realize, but is no less repellent for it. He wonders aloud about these "murderers" who go around on the streets in broad daylight, and imagines the murderers in the prisons being released, all at once, to join them. It's not the same to read about murder as to actually know a murderer, he says. They leave, but later Alexandre returns, alone this time, and talks more with Veronika. He mentions her drinking, which makes her defensive. They remember their first meeting. And why didn't he sleep with her, she wants to know, the first time she offered?

HE TALKS ABOUT GILBERTE. How do people leave each other, Alexandre asks. And, stranger still, why do they intervene to force what time will inevitably accomplish anyway, binding or separating them? (Léaud looks straight at the camera.) He says he used to fight with Gilberte. Once he hit her so hard — Jesus — that she looked "like Frankenstein" when they made love. When she told him she was pregnant he left in a rage, then realized how profoundly he wanted her and the baby, but returned to find her gone. She'd had an abortion, and said she didn't love him anymore. How was this the woman who asked him what novel he was living in, or did she mean more by that question than we could have possibly understood? He says he became like a character "in a bad film." His face is rigid, steeped in bitterness. Veronika listens with tears shining in her eyes.

HER FRIEND ARRIVES, SOME other men join them, Alexandre leaves the café. She comes chasing after him: "I love you, and I want to fuck you again." Does fuck mean fuck once, or does "I want to fuck you" mean something like "I want to know you," the verb indefinite, open-ended? What lies beyond a single fuck? And where will they do it—in her little garret? He seeks out girls with apartments, he says, since he doesn't have one of his own. She likes to fuck Arabs and Jews, is her appalling retort, she adores "aliens." She wants him to come do it now but he says no, it will have to wait until later that night.

THEY'RE TOGETHER IN THE hallway of the hospital. The intervening hours have disappeared without even shuffling the players. And yet they were apart, and he asks her—they're in her room now, it's as sordid as she'd warned—what she's done in the time since they saw each other that afternoon. Called someone up, she tells him, and "got fucked." Hadn't she told him she wanted a cock? A little reverie: "It's nice to sleep feeling a cock, even soft, against your ass." Is she making him jealous? No, excited. They mash their faces together. Sex in the hospital. What did she do with her lover? "He said, 'Undress, do what I like.'" "What's that?" "I won't tell." "Then do it to me." "No, it's too tiring." He keeps guessing—we've already guessed. What did she use? Her mouth...

WHAT'S DELICIOUS ABOUT A man? His ankle boots. His small pectoral muscles. His aggrieved pout. How serious he is about communism. His big nose ("Is my nose too big?"—Léaud in *Masculin Féminin*).

"He yawned. He had finished the day and he had also finished with his youth. Various well-bred moralities had already discreetly offered him their services: disillusioned epicureanism, smiling tolerance, resignation, common sense stoicism—all the aids whereby a man may savour, minute by minute, like a connoisseur, the failure of a life."—Jean-Paul Sartre, *The Age of Reason*.

Am I supposed to identify with someone in this movie? I'm nothing like Léaud, I want to shout, but there is something about his tetchiness and his pomposity, so definitive of the masculine surface. I identify most of all with the threesome: their fascination with doom: the doom of telling the truth about desire: how it can't stop moving on: how that is its nature: how to deny it is entirely possible, of course, but nevertheless how to do so is to swallow, with each successive denial, a spoonful of ash.

BUT COME ON, WHY do you look so serious?

MORNING, SHE'S IN HER nurse's whites, she leaves him in bed but soon he's walking out into the bright morning street like anyone who finds himself in a room no longer occupied by the lover of the night before. At home, Marie's awake. They exchange a significant glance, he crawls into bed. Fade out. People—the few one sees in summer, in the empty city—ask me what I'm writing about, and I can barely say it aloud (let alone write it in a grant proposal): *The Mother and the Whore*. Are those words in quotation marks? Is this somehow the title Alexandre would choose? Is this a movie about the strictures of categories, or their unraveling? Sometimes we find ourselves in a room we've never been in before, with someone who's fucked elsewhere that same day and tantalizes us with the tale. Sometimes a person takes us in, after such adventures, and rolls over to make space in the bed where we collapse, spent and spit out by the desire that has been using us as a pawn or vessel. Do these acts presuppose a role in relation to the one who is tantalized or comforted? The streets aren't really full of murderers. But the streets are rich with mirrors, and walking out, we may wish to avoid them and the way they everywhere infinitize the world— unbearably, if the world they reflect is unbearable.

THE BY-NOW FAMILIAR PATTERN: having given in to Veronika, Alexandre must make up with Marie. He shows up at her dress shop in his dark sunglasses, goes in, she's there in her dark sunglasses. There's a customer; Marie shows the woman to the dressing room and Alexandre watches idly in a mirror tilted such that he can watch the woman pull off her top and try on a blouse. After the woman pays and leaves, Marie beckons Alexandre to the back. She's set aside a new scarf for him, no sooner has she tied it around his neck than she's in his arms again. These goings-on—are they possible? Commonplace? Or not? Merely fantasy? Does someone know for sure?

THEY'RE IN BED, ASLEEP, when Veronika calls. Turns out "elle est ivre"—I know that one—she's drunk in a nightclub somewhere. Alexandre puts her off but, awake now, lights a cigarette. Léaud has an inoculation scar on his right shoulder. "She's a bit lost, huh?" he asks Marie, whose expression says she can hardly believe he's just figuring this out. He sits up, alert. Working people seem so stable, he reflects, but if this woman gets wasted and calls people's homes in the middle of the night, perhaps other workers are also wavering, and coming un-glued. Why does anyone go to work anyway, how can they keep it up when they could walk away, anytime, for "everything...nothing." He recalls driving on a highway between Marseilles and Lyon and falling asleep at the wheel, not waking up until the car bumped the guard rail. The highway, in that moment, became a vision of itself 1,000 years in the future, "cracked and fissured" and overgrown with weeds, a ruin of a lost civilization, now traversed by vagabonds "like the end of a Chaplin film." He makes lists of the things that will be lost, and keeps coming back to "cinema," until finally: "Maybe someone very old, really old, will still remember, and tell the youth about the movies, about pictures that moved and talked, and the young won't under-stand." But Alexandre is already on to the break-down of social classes, thugs who stab people in the back in the street, and then, to Marie, "when I make love with you, I think only of death, of earth, of ashes." Marie, bless her: "You never told me that." And he, sarcastically, "Why? Do you see rivers, rushing waterfalls?"

WHAT TO MAKE OF Alexandre's well-developed death drive? He sees suicides and murderers everywhere he goes. He's made love to Veronika, that passive, inscrutable creature, sure, but even with Marie, Marie the shop owner, Marie the cook, Marie the one who laughs in the middle of their arguments so that the tension falls away like water from a body emerging from a bath, even with her he thinks of death, he is plunged into the suffocating earth, he watches everything burn. Eustache's autofiction writes its own macabre ending. Will it be, as in *Last Tango in Paris*, a violent extinction? Will it be the end of "Sarrasine," where the survivor, relieved of obsession's grip, lingers to haunt the baffled, still-entangled living? Will it be, as in Proust, a confrontation with the cage of subjectivity from which we cannot see others, or even the estranged other selves we've been and will inevitably become? But Proust discovers that his art makes him more aware, that the echoes and patterns he detects and to which he gives name are keys to the understanding that surpasses his corporeal life. Or so he claims, though who could be better at depicting the wretched moment when desire wears us like a glove or puppet.

THE PHONE WAKES THEM again at four. Veronika again, drunker still, and coming over, though they ask her not to. Alexandre admires her determination: "I don't like dignity." Veronika knocks, Marie is the one to get up (naked) and go to the door, Veronika is there with a taxi driver she has no money to pay. Inside at last, she kneels on the bed and regards the poor couple she's woken. "Shitty old Alexandre," she drawls. He barely raises his eyes to her. "Rotten old Marie." "And you, sweet, tender, pure Veronika," Marie shoots back, jolting their visitor. "I'm completely rotten," she offers, chastened. "I've drunk a maximum tonight." She loves this word, *maximum*. (At some level, the French are unbelievably uncool.) She undresses and climbs into bed, kisses them each in turn. It's not quite the release we expected, though it's crossed our minds. Not quite the sudden key to their problems turning in the lock. Alexandre watches, sullen, then dives atop both women, only to have Veronika slip away and say she wants to watch Marie and him fuck. Fade out. Threesomes are notoriously unstable. Online I find a photo of the three actors on set, looking deliriously happy together, and another of the three of them laughing and smiling with Eustache at a café. The poster for this movie is the three leads: their faces. It hangs on the wall of the awful dad's apartment, I remember, in *The Squid and the Whale*.

IN THE MORNING, VERONIKA tells Alexandre, "I'm crazy about you." They kiss across a still-sleeping Marie. Next scene: they're at a store, descending an escalator—glorious cinematic trope—on their way to buy liquor for a party at the apartment. Alexandre is ebullient, filling a shopping cart with booze. On the way out he bangs into another cart, looks up, it's Gilberte and her fiancé—coy Eustache himself, in the briefest of cameos—passing the other way. Still, irrepressible, Alexandre bursts in Marie's door with the shopping bag handles between his teeth. "Anything to nibble on?" he asks Marie. "No." He'll spend the whole long scene ahead trying to score a snack. It's both an intellectual commonplace and a leitmotif of this movie to say that we are discontinuous—far less whole than we like to pretend. But if we really believed that of each other, how much more forgiving would we have to be? Marie tells Alexandre that Phillipe is invited. "I won't stand for it!" he yells, and storms out. She comes out to the car where he sits with Veronika, and berates and spits on him. He goes back up and trades hyper-articulate barbs with Marie until the only other partygoer finally slips away, aghast. Back to the three of them, then, the click of liquor pouring into glasses. Alexandre checks that no one is hungry (though he is, for the rabbit in mustard sauce that was supposed to be dinner) and makes an unconvincing speech about how ugly scenes are the best appetite suppressant. And what can cure the tiresome disease of possessiveness, he asks the

nurse. She replies with a terrible pun: Vitamin M
("aime"—love).

SLOW-MOTION CHAOS, A SQUALL of indecision, we're adrift in a maximum of cinema. Veronika makes up Marie while Alexandre puts on a somber record. The women whisper and giggle. Then Veronika makes up Alexandre, who pouts. When she's through, they admire him, and advise him to go get fucked up the ass by some interested man. "You know it's your problem," Marie adds, i.e. that he's averse to the idea. Threatened, he lies stiff in bed, muttering "leave me alone" while Veronika warns him to "cut the bullshit. You're the happiest man in the world. You're in the sack with two chicks who love you." She cuddles up to him, whispers "fuck me...fuck me...", his resistance fades and when he leaps on top of her, Marie draws close, only to be brushed away more than once by Veronika. Marie leaps up, goes to the bathroom, emerges with a bottle of pills, and promptly swallows them all. Alexandre forces her to throw them up in the bathroom—off-camera—then gets back in bed with Veronika. He touches her, she's appalled by his *sang froid*, he turns away, she starts caressing him, he's on top of her again, Marie reappears and throws them both out.

A MOTHER: THE SOURCE of care, which is to say, someone who understands that these words just came out of their own accord, expressing themselves. I had meant to say something different. Abject, she harbors my disavowal, it's enough for her that it's mine.

A whore: someone obliged to grant another the power to fulfill their particular desire, which is to say, someone obliged to accept that such desires exist, even if they seem shameful, even if we ourselves aren't desirable, or don't feel we could be.

A mother: the feathery edge of absorption and revolt, a partner willing to let us test, with them at the other end, the elasticity of human tether.

A whore: a lie in darkness through which a desperate supplicant peers for a flash of involuntary truth—the stainless-steel armature over which he believes, sadly, this bruised organic world to be loosely draped.

So who's who? Or are these roles to pull on and slough off like silks, like furs? Could Eustache traffic in more than identifications, binaries, and programs? Or did he just want to place a heavy pause before the answers to those habitual but impossible questions: What are you watching? What are you writing about?

I KNOW THERE WAS a time when I found it all great fun: this movie, and *Husbands*, and *Last Tango in Paris*, and *Les Valseuses (Going Places)*, and *La Collectionneuse*. All the men...the ribald and questing and troubled men, the libertines and brutes and hypocrites. A whole film swirling around the face of a desirable and desired woman, if not on screen, then in the imagination of the man watching. As if Lacan's famous decree did not also contain a riddle: "The only thing one can be guilty of is giving ground relative to one's desire."

GO EASY ON ME, mother me: I was looking for something better, more free and alive than the role I'd been handed: clumsy and inarticulate thing. But now the surge of defiance sits uneasily in my belly, I know what debris looks like, and how shiny it was at the start, and I know that the movies know too, and knew it all along, but I had to live a lot in order to learn how to watch them, rather than watching them, as Alexandre says misleadingly, in order to learn how to live.

"YOU HAVE SHITTY RELATIONSHIPS with women."
Alexandre sits silently, while Veronika sips a suc-
cession of whiskeys in the café to which they've
been banished. "But at times, you're nice, you
seem to love people. But you have shitty relationships." She guesses he must have driven Gilberte
crazy, since she must have really loved him as she,
Veronika, really loves him, though she knows, and
keeps saying, that he's an asshole. Love is almost
simple. She gets up, tells him to order her another
whiskey. This movie is drinks, records, and talk: an
urban trinity. He orders two more. "I thought of
you in the toilet," she tells him when she returns. "A
bit of graffiti: 'My passion opens out on death like a
window on a courtyard.' And someone had added,
'Jump, Narcissus!'" Think of Phillips again, who
says the superego hasn't much imagination, chastis-
es us always in the same narrow terms, and tells us
that its adversaries—celebration and praise—are
weaknesses, so that our sense of celebration with-
ers, until we forget how to praise at all. And, I'd
add, how to die, since praise is a kind of benedic-
tion on the world and, as such, an admission that it
doesn't require our presence to continue.

THE THREE OF THEM in the apartment again. Out come the corks, but only after Veronika gives Alexandre a shot of Vitamin C in his "lovely veins." She remembers there was a nurse who healed all the gorgeous patients, while she herself always got the ones ravaged by cancer. The first dead person she ever saw was her grandfather — she was fifteen — and although he'd been a cruel man, he was also a self-styled mystic, and a "maximum of priests" came to pay their respects, and her grandmother, who had been the primary recipient of the old man's cruelty, swore she saw the body move. But Veronika saw that it did not move. This is the sole childhood detail we are given, about any of them. It's as if they've all come from nowhere, already complete. It's hard enough to live in the city without having to worry about everyone's backstory, sisters or brothers, or much beyond "troubled," beyond hungry, beyond came out of murk and afraid that to it they must return unless a stroke of luck waits down the dark street, or rings the phone at dawn.

MARIE AND ALEXANDRE LOOK fed up. Veronika keeps talking. Alexandre goes and sprays the aerosol over his face again. Another gratingly racist moment, Veronika and Marie talk about how Marie's darker features, as they call them, don't fit Alexandre's predilection for blondes. Othering is contagious. Veronika rambles about how Alexandre—he looks miserable—will remember this triumphant moment with pleasure when he's old and in a wheelchair (as if she wasn't invoking the fate that frightens him most). But this makes her think about his conquests, about "fuck stories" as a category, and the idea, perhaps, that we fuck to fill ourselves with such stories, and that each fuck becomes just another one to keep and to tell. She fears Alexandre thinks she's such a story, that he's found a "whorish Gilberte" in her. "But," she asserts—are these Eustache's words? Lebrun's?—"there are no whores. For me, a girl who lets anyone fuck her, any way, is no whore. For me, there are no whores, that's all." And a married woman who dreams of getting fucked by the electrician or some movie star is no whore either, she insists. "There are just cunts, genitals." I look over my shoulder, in the library. I have hoarded, it's true, my share of fuck stories ("As if the act of having sex had a meaning/Beyond/Recalling" —Jack Spicer). I have played them on repeat in the slow-motion video player of my memory, and wondered what the feeling in them became, where it went, if it added up, if it lingers somewhere, if it changed anything. And what's porn but the fuck stories of the world, encoded so often with the struggle over who gets to look at, record, and define a naked act.

AMONG THOSE PAST LOVES: the cineaste. Whenever she tested me, as though casually, with a question about the movies, I inevitably failed. Her elusiveness was perfected in her commitment to an art form that, because it unfolds in real time, means that if you wish to catch up with the expert you must devote every hour they have already devoted, all the while knowing that in those same hours they themselves watch more, adding to their surpassing knowledge and maintaining their unchanging lead from your pursuit. Her interest in the form went deeper than expertise. To watch movies, after all, is to live both in and apart from the pure duration of one's own time passing. The replayability of film was a kind of ontological position for her. Didn't she say, bluntly, when I told her how much a certain night had meant, "I know," as if she contemplated me and the feelings that tore me apart from a distance, and merely witnessed my drama unfold as she might regard an obscure French film she'd seen twenty times? With the implication that, just as she'd seen so much that I hadn't, she had experienced all this pain already, and could no longer be touched by it, as if she watched a movie that once made her weep and now noticed a woman's hat in the background of a climactic shot or enjoyed a quirky translation in the subtitles—while I, watching for the first time beside her, was moved to shattering sobs by the plot.

THERE IS ONLY VERONIKA'S face, now: her head lolling against the wall behind, her large eyes whose makeup runs with her tears down wide cheeks toward her dimpled chin. "Why so much importance on these fuck stories?" It's been five years, she says, since she lost her virginity at age twenty. Since then, "I took a maximum of lovers, and got fucked." But it's all shit. "Just one thing is beautiful...fucking because you're so in love you want to make a baby who looks like you...and otherwise it's something sordid...you should only fuck if you're in love...I've been fucked like a whore...a couple that doesn't want a baby is not a couple, it's shit, it's anything, dust..." All the frisson of Veronika saying this, so that what had seemed like her sexual casualness is revealed, rather, as her numb acceptance of the "liberated" sexual world in which she's forced to exist. Has the Left ever stopped being surprised to have its gifts returned unopened like this, spurned by the values of a nurse? Longing and prejudice and piety still skulk around, in this time in which we find ourselves, when people seem afraid of each other and unsure of how close they are, how much they can ask of anyone, what the purpose or meaning of their frenetic coupling or exhaustion with coupling might be, and who will take care of them when they're sick. All that porn and online dating and virtualized fantasy, all those botched relationships and troughs of anomie, all the diminishments of age in this empire of youth, sputtered-out revolutions and social programs and daily reports of suffering at the hands of the unstoppably cynical and corrupt. Marguerite Duras: "It's between men and women that imagination is at its strongest. And it's there that they're separated by a frigidity which women increasingly invoke and which paralyses the men who desire them." Tender or violent—an impasse either way. A baby who looks like you. Sex in the hospital. Binary as ton of bricks.

WHAT DO THE MOVIES say about taking no for an answer? Brando chases Schneider in the streets, pretends to let her go, waits till she goes into her building, grabs the door, runs breathless up the staircase that winds around the shaft through which her elevator car ascends. She makes the apartment, tries to shut the door, he wedges his body in the opening before she can get it closed. Then, just like that, he's calm—there's nowhere for her to escape. Plops her father's cap on his head—dad was a military commander in French Algeria—and mock salutes. He tells her he loves her. He asks her name. She has taken the military pistol from the dresser drawer, and shoots him in the gut. He lurches out to the balcony to die. He's wanted to die all along, ever since his wife committed suicide, an act for which he knows he must in some way be responsible. Recall that Léaud falls out the window, offscreen, at the end of *Masculin Féminin*, a movie whose title, perhaps, would have us interrogate the apparent equality between the genders, a very French premise belied by the reality of what we've seen. Men are hungry ghosts.

THE THOUGHT: WHAT IF it never ends, this movie whose structure is infinite dialectic? But incredibly, the end is near. Silhouettes listen to a requiem, still and silent, Marie with her fingers templed, Veronika a chalice in her lap. Alexandre apart, scribbling something at the high desk in the far corner. "This is cheerful!" Oh, Marie. "Enough's enough"—Veronika, who asks Alexandre to take her home. He moves to obey. Marie puts on Edith Piaf—at last—"Les Amants de Paris," a song about the strange lovers of Paris, millions of them, and how they have always used the singer's ballads, as in some lover's discourse described by Barthes, to heighten their own ultimately commonplace adventures. Farewell, Marie.

THEY PULL UP TO the hospital. (Remember, Alexandre *borrowed* this car in the first scene.) I wish they'd shot the whole movie in sequence—a wish to see precisely what Eustache warns will never be visible: the physiognomy of consequence. Alexandre runs and slides across institutional floors in pursuit of Veronika, who stalks to her room, only to stop and yell, "You disgust me!"—she even whacks him with her purse—"you disgust me! I may be pregnant by you. I love you. You can't even let the people you love be drunk." A doctor peers down the corridor at the ruckus. Alexandre lets her go, struts his little Léaud-strut out to the car, stops abruptly, runs back. In her room, she's in a snow-white robe, she laughs an unhinged laugh and falls onto the bed as he stands over her demanding to know if she loves him. More important, will she marry him? She's sick, she says, pregnant and drunk and about to throw up, if he wants to marry her he should make himself useful and get a basin. It's a hospital. He hands one to her, she yells "Turn around!" and he falls backward to the floor in front of her little refrigerator and winces, squeamish or empathetic, at her retching (eerie echo of the offscreen sounds of Marie choking out the pills). An ambivalent expression drifts over his face. Fade out. No music. The end.

ALL THESE IDEAS AND positions, reversals and regrets, all this talk. Of the public, Eustache told an
interviewer, "When they think they enter the film,
it is a trap, they don't enter...when the film finishes
they are perhaps discontent to have remained on
the outside, then they try to understand something,
but there is nothing to understand, everything has
been said." And yet I drift over to my laptop, to
type, to email Rachel, to tell her that I miss her, to
try to think it through.

AND AFTER ALL, MAYBE the obvious thought about the movie is the most devastating one. Eustache made a film, once, about the slaughter of a pig, and his interest was in showing the event rather than framing it with documentary conventions. He made another film, *Numéro zéro*, in which his grandmother tells her life story while we observe. Likewise he turned his camera on adolescence, on the landscapes of the south, on raconteurs and their tales. He was a recorder more than a philosopher, in other words—and he always says so. The harrowing truth about *The Mother and the Whore* is that, beneath all the flourish and cogitation, he simply lived it, the chaos and hysteria on screen is just someone's actual, demonstrable mess. As Eustache claimed, "I wrote this screenplay because I loved a woman who had left me." Barthes's sense of the lover's story was that it had to traffic in codes and figures belonging to no one but recognizable to everyone, and that each lover made a kind of path through these inherited figures without, at any point, rising above them. The string of episodes, arranged horizontally, that make up any given love story can thus be reported without disrupting the overall order of things, so that "the love story...is the tribute the lover must pay to the world in order to be reconciled with it." And yet, for Eustache—or for Catherine Garnier, it seems— there could be no reconciliation. The code dissolves, the figures crumble. Like Werther or Sarrasine or Emma Bovary, they could not survive the tale. What kind of novel did they think they were in?

HEADING FROM MY BED-STUY apartment to Manhattan in the sticky 90-degree heat. On the subway I re-read Tom Wolfe's *The Electric Kool-Aid Acid Test*—it's been years—and discover an amazing chapter about two-thirds in, that takes place while Kesey is hiding out in Mexico because the cops are after him for possession. The Pranksters are coming unhinged in his absence. They hold an Acid Test in Watts, the first one with the actual kool aid, in 1966, with all the delirious hope of that moment, and, in a rare gesture in the book, Wolfe cedes his authorial voice to let a woman named Clair Brush give a verbatim account of her first time taking acid—by mistake—and how a friend held her tightly, and she felt she merged with him so totally that she feels bonded to him even decades later, and she talks about the wondrous experience of the blacklight that turned her skin a velvety purple she still sometimes wishes it really was. At one point she hears a woman shout, not un-Veronika-like, at her boyfriend: "Who cares, Ray? Sex! Ray! Sex! Who cares!" The book, this part especially, makes me remember my own trips, the sublime afternoons when I felt close to people and profoundly safe, and every pose and stricture seemed ridiculous and easily banished. Or the bad ones, nights when the feeling I now call claustrophobia came over me, a tightness in the chest, a presentiment of the suffocation that will surely craze us on the inexorably-approaching day when the world retracts from us its breath. The awful—erotic?—moment of true fear arriving, and whatever comforts we've contrived to hold it off are useless: the fear is too nimble and enormous, it devours possibility, it turns time to stone, it even appears sometimes—as if innocuously—in love songs, under its ancient and formerly solemn name, which is fate.

PEOPLE ARE COMING DOWN into the station wet as I'm going up and out. Under an awning stand a cop and a few people in shorts and t-shirts waiting out the downpour, inspecting their phones. I brought an umbrella, so I set out towards the park. The sky is full of brown and gray smudges of clouds, the trunks of the trees in Washington Square Park are shining. Already the rain is abating. A mother and father not-very-happily watch their perhaps 15-year-old daughter take photos of their perhaps 13-year-old daughter in "sexy" poses by the spraying fountain. A toddler runs by, feet slapping the wet cobbles, his father chasing behind. A man stops me for directions to Christopher Street. I indicate west, he turns to go, then stops and turns back to me. "My sister was killed in there"—he's pointing down LaGuardia toward the site of the World Trade Center—"after giving bone marrow to me. And now that thing's there." He means the so-called Freedom Tower. I say I'm sorry. He shrugs and leaves for good. I go into the library. Duration's not a void, it's a sharp wire. I lost two decades here, to uncertainty. I'm afraid I'm going to lose several more—and find myself on their far side, only a cut away.

I LOOK AT THE illustrations in Phillipon's book: Eustache busy and smiling, the actors in character or loitering on set. If there's a new world growing inside this one, I can't see it, but I'd like to go there if you can take me, I can come apart if necessary, I can fit through, I don't need to bring these grasping hands, those numbing drinks and jittery smokes, time is running out, I want to see the new words that wait, shining, for our voices to speak them, I want to go back to the night when it all started, and this time not say *care*, or *need*, or *love*, and find out if we could emerge the next morning not having made one another, in the intervening darkness that passed like a movie or a dream, somehow even more terribly alone.

Acknowledgments

This work was blessed with the most insightful and generous first readers: Carley Moore, Sara Jane Stoner, Anna Gurton-Wachter, Alex Baker, Gabriel Kruis, and Dave Smoota Smith. And it was written with the voices of dear friends and collaborators in mind: Madeleine George, erica kaufman, Stacy Szymaszek, David Buuck, Simone White, Ali Power, Litia Perta, Stephanie Hopkins, Emily Reilly, John Coletti, Anselm Berrigan, Dawn Lundy Martin, Jess Arndt, Judah Rubin, Brendan Lorber, Ariel Friedman, Amy Touchette, Karen Weiser, Ted Dodson, Dan Schwartz, Dia Felix, Karen Lepri, Bill Webb, Alexis Almeida, Carolyn Bush, and Adjua Gargi Nzinga Greaves. I couldn't have hoped for more brilliant editors than Anna Moschovakis, Lee Norton, and Kyra Simone, or for more care and expertise than I found at UDP. This book is for my mother and my late father. It is for Malka Longabucco and the boundless inspiration and joy she brings. It is for Rachel Valinsky, with love. Our ongoing conversation is at its heart.